KING JOHN
and MAGNA CARTA

by L. DU GARDE PEACH, M.A., Ph.D., D.Litt.

with illustrations by JOHN KENNEY

Publishers: Wills & Hepworth Ltd., Loughborough

First published 1969   ©   *Printed in England*

KING JOHN and MAGNA CARTA

King John was probably the worst king ever to mount the English throne. He was cruel and treacherous, a boastful coward; mean and deceitful as a man, utterly untrustworthy as a king. He died loathed by everyone who knew him, regretted by none.

Yet because he was so bad, we probably owe more to him than to any other English monarch from Alfred to Elizabeth I. If John had been a good king, the freedoms which we in England enjoy today might have been delayed for centuries.

It was because John was so evil that the nobles, the Church, and the common people of England forced him to affix his seal to the document known as Magna Carta, or the Great Charter.

John was the favourite son of King Henry II, and the younger brother of Richard the Lion Heart, about whom you may have read in another book in this series. Although Henry gave John everything he asked for, including the revenue from six English counties, he rebelled against Henry and treasonably joined the French against his own country. His attempted rebellion was not successful, but his treachery is said to have broken his father's heart.

John's elder brother, Richard, was King of England for ten years but spent only seven months in his kingdom. The rest of the time he was leading the famous crusades to recover Jerusalem.

The people of England had no love for a monarch whose only interest in them was the money he forced them to pay in taxes. When Richard, trying to return home across Europe, was imprisoned by the Emperor of Germany, John thought that this was his chance to make himself King. He sent a letter to the Emperor, asking him to keep Richard away from England as long as possible.

The Emperor had other ideas. Richard was worth money, and he demanded £100,000 as a ransom. This was a very large sum for a poor country like England. It was raised and paid because although Richard was a bad king, everybody knew that John would be a worse one.

John had been a traitor to his brother and his king: now he became even more contemptible. He pretended that he was sorry for what he had done, and begged Richard to forgive him. No-one would have been surprised if Richard had decided to execute him for treason. Instead, he forgave John and named him as his heir.

When Richard I died in the year 1199, John hastened to have himself crowned as King of England. Nobody wanted him, but they knew that without a king of some sort there would be civil war between the nobles, and everybody would suffer.

There was another reason why John wanted to be crowned as soon as possible. Another brother, Geoffrey of Anjou, had been older than John. This brother had died twelve years earlier, and left a son, Arthur, who had a better claim to the throne than John.

At that time a large part of France was ruled by England, and the French King Philip now decided to support the claim of Arthur, who was only twelve years old, against John. Soon there was fighting all over France.

There was no real loyalty to anyone. The French nobles had no wish to be ruled by anybody, least of all by a boy of twelve, but they saw an opportunity for plunder. So did King Philip. As an excuse he recognised Arthur as the Duke of Normandy and over-lord of Anjou and Aquitaine, titles which belonged to the King of England. John raised an army and sailed for France.

John had only one friend in France, his mother, the dowager Queen Eleanor. In spite of his wickedness, he had always been her favourite son. When John was obliged to return to England, she carried on the war. Soon she found herself besieged by the army of King Philip and the boy Arthur, in the castle of Mirabeau.

She sent word to John to come to her help. By making a rapid return to France, and a forced march across country, he surprised the French army. Arthur was taken prisoner.

In those days a boy had very little hope of growing up if he happened to be an obstacle to a king's ambition. Arthur was doomed the moment he fell into his uncle's hands.

John could not help being treacherous, even when it was not necessary. At first he pretended to be the kind uncle. He promised that no harm should come to Arthur if he would give up his claim to the throne. Arthur refused, and soon found himself in a dungeon. No-one knows what happened to him after that. All that is certain is that he was murdered, either by King John's orders, or by John himself. He was never heard of again.

John had been hated and despised before the disappearance of Arthur; now he was regarded as a murderer. Not that murderers were uncommon in the thirteenth century, but John, a king, had murdered his own nephew. Not until Richard III murdered his two young nephews in the Tower of London, almost three centuries later, has a King of England been so reviled.

The news of this terrible act spread across Europe. Any followers John had on the continent quickly turned against him.

It almost seemed as though John was determined to do everything he could to make as many enemies as possible. In France he had seen a very beautiful young girl named Isabella, the daughter of the Count of Angouleme. Although she was engaged to be married to a young French nobleman, John sent a party of men-at-arms and carried her off by force.

In order to marry Isabella, he had to get rid of his wife Avice, who was the heiress of the Earl of Gloucester. As even John hesitated to murder the Queen of England, he arranged a divorce. This meant that he aroused the fury of the nobles of both France and England.

In the thirteenth century, all western Europe was governed by what was known as the 'feudal' system. This meant that every man owed allegiance to the man immediately above him: the common people to the knights, the knights to the nobles, and the nobles to the King. This was because in time of trouble people needed to be protected by someone more powerful than themselves.

This protection went with the land they occupied. In return each had to give service in war and peace to the landowner.

As King John was also the Duke of Normandy, as well as holding other French estates and titles, he was what was called a vassal of the King of France, in addition to being King of England.

King Philip of France summoned John as his vassal to appear before him to answer for his action in carrying off the young French heiress. John was doubtful about putting himself in the power of the French King. So he sent two envoys, Hugh de Burgh and the Bishop of Ely, to ask if he would be given a safe conduct. Philip replied that he could certainly come in safety, but whether he would be allowed to return depended on the verdict. John very wisely stayed at home.

Philip at once declared that John must forfeit all French lands and titles, which meant that the war was renewed. Very few men, except paid mercenaries, were prepared to fight for John. Soon all the vast estates in France, which Henry II had left to his sons, were lost. Today only the Channel Islands remain of what once belonged to England.

Not content with losing all his French possessions, John now quarrelled with the Pope.

The quarrel arose out of the election of an Archbishop. The monks of Canterbury chose one of themselves, and England being at that time a Catholic country, the newly-chosen Archbishop immediately set off for Rome to obtain the Pope's approval.

King John was furious. He insisted that only the monarch could elect the Archbishop of Canterbury. With his armed followers at his back, he went to Canterbury and summoned all the monks together. Faced by an angry king and surrounded by armed men with drawn swords, the terrified monks agreed to the King's choice, and a second priest hurried off to Rome. When the two priests stood before the Pope, awaiting his decision, he declared that neither of them had been properly elected, and himself named a third, Stephen Langton.

16

The Pope had no right to elect the Archbishop of Canterbury, and King John stubbornly refused to accept his choice. The Pope was equally stubborn. When he wrote to the King insisting on Langton's installation as Archbishop, John refused even to answer the letter.

The monks of Canterbury were in a very difficult position. As priests of the Catholic Church, they were obliged to obey the Pope. When they met and agreed to accept Archbishop Langton, John sent men-at-arms and drove them out of the country.

The Pope's reply was to place England under an interdict. This meant that all religious services in the country would cease, and all churches would be closed. No church bells could be rung, and no ceremonies performed. Priests refused to let anyone into the churches.

The Pope ordered three bishops to inform John of his decree. As they stood trembling before the uncontrolled fury of the King, John shouted angrily, "If any priest dares to proclaim the interdict, I will cut off his nose and send him back to the Pope without it!" The bishops were driven from his presence, but on the appointed day they proclaimed the interdict, and very wisely fled across the Channel. Others followed, and soon only one bishop was left in England.

The Pope now proceeded to excommunicate John. This meant that he was utterly cast out from the Church, and that he was no longer fit to be a king. In the same proclamation the Pope granted the Kingdom of England to Philip of France.

The Pope had no more right to give away the English Crown than he had to appoint an Archbishop. John took no notice of the threat. But he was now very much alone. The nobles and the Church were all against him, and the common people hated him because the taxes he imposed upon them made it almost impossible for them to live.

Only by employing mercenary soldiers was John able to rule the country. He did so by seizing the castles of the nobles and holding their children as hostages.

Some of the nobles remained at the court rather than risk the King's vengeance. Others dared to defy him. One of them, named de Braose, escaped and fled the country, only to die in exile. This so infuriated John, and so vile was his nature, that he cast de Braose's innocent wife and children into prison, where they were slowly starved to death. Others were brutally murdered. No man, rich or poor, was safe.

In obedience to the Pope, the French King gathered an army to invade England. John realised that he had no-one on whom he could rely to fight the French. A story is told of how, in his craven fear, he did something which showed the kind of man he was.

It is related that he sent an ambassador to the Emir of Cordova, who was, of course, a Mohammedan, begging for his help. Cordova was a little state held by the Moors in the southern part of what is now Spain. In return, John promised not only to pay a yearly tribute to the Emir, but himself to renounce the Christian religion and become a Mohammedan.

When the Emir heard that the King of England was ready to declare England a vassal of Cordova, he was filled with scorn. "Away with you!" he said. "Your King is unworthy to be a vassal of Cordova. He is a coward and a weakling, and his infamy stinks in my nostrils!"

It is not recorded what John said when the embassy returned to England. To be scorned by the ruler of such a small state was to sink low indeed.

John, King of the country which under his famous brother Richard Coeur de Lion had been feared from one end of Europe to the other, was to sink lower yet.

He had managed to gather an army in Kent, but he was very doubtful of its loyalty. He was terrified by the prospect of an invasion by the French King, and he racked his brains to think of some way of preventing it. At last he devised what seemed to him a very good plan. John was never wise, but he was cunning. His new plan meant swallowing any pride he might have had, but that was not a thing to worry King John of England.

He decided to grovel to the Pope, to receive Stephen Langton as the Archbishop of Canterbury, and to call back all the exiled bishops and clergy. He hoped that by doing so the Pope would order Philip to cancel the threatened invasion. So he summoned the Abbot of Beaulieu, one of the few remaining churchmen in the country, and sent him to Rome to open negotiations with the Pope.

Even more afraid of his own army than of the French, he galloped north with a few retainers and took refuge in Nottingham Castle.

Nobody ever trusted John, the Pope least of all. He decided to send a Papal Legate to England to receive John's humiliating submission.

The Papal Legate was a Cardinal named Pandulph. The King met him at Dover, and the Cardinal smilingly described the preparations which Philip had made for the invasion of England. He stressed the Pope's readiness to lift the interdict, only hinting at what might happen if John refused the conditions attached to his forgiveness.

It was enough to frighten the King. He promised to do everything the Pope wished, but without any intention of keeping his promise if conditions changed.

He went further. In a document to which he set his seal, he promised to give and confer on the Pope and his Catholic successors, the whole Kingdom of England. "Henceforth," he said, "we hold it as a fief." In other words, John gave England to the Pope. He knelt at the feet of the Papal Legate and handed him the Crown of England, receiving it back as a vassal of the Pope. He also laid a bag of money at the Legate's feet as a tribute. Pandulph showed his opinion of the cowardly King by scattering the money across the floor with his foot.

Never has a King of England been so humiliated, before or since. John had hoped that by gaining the forgiveness of the Pope he could not only win his support but gain a triumph over the nobles who were opposing him at home. So long as the interdict and the excommunication lasted, the nobles were relieved of their allegiance to him. Now, if they continued to disobey him, they would be traitors.

He had also hoped that the threatened invasion would be called off. Philip had gathered his army at the Pope's request to punish King John: now that the offence was forgiven, the army would, he hoped, be disbanded.

He reckoned without Philip. It cost a great deal of money to assemble an army, and Philip had no intention of wasting it. Prevented by the Pope from invading England, he marched north against the Count of Flanders, who had allied himself with John.

John's cunning had removed the fear of invasion, but it created more trouble at home. The news of the shameful scene with the Papal Legate united the nobles and commoners as they had never been united before. Everywhere he went John was met by sullen crowds.

John now had his one and quite undeserved success. As the French army marched along the coast roads of France and Belgium, the French fleet sailed parallel with it, a few miles off shore. An English nobleman, the Earl of Salisbury, gathered a fleet of English ships and caught up with it near Damme, then a sea-port.

In the engagement which followed, the French fleet was utterly destroyed. As it was the only means of provisioning the French army, Philip was obliged to retreat.

All danger of invasion now past, John decided to invade France in an attempt to recover his lost possessions. He summoned all the nobles of England to report with their retainers, and he raised levies in the shires. But many of the northern nobles failed to respond and John crossed to France with such men as he had.

He had formed an alliance with the ruler of Germany, who with the Count of Flanders was to attack Philip from the north, whilst John advanced from the south. At first this plan was successful, but in a battle at Bouvines John's allies were disastrously defeated. John returned to England with his army, without having achieved anything.

John, already hated and despised, now landed in England defeated and humiliated. He returned to a country which was being driven towards open revolution by the conditions in which the people existed.

The villeins or serfs lived in squalor and misery. Their huts were built of wattles woven together and daubed with clay, with earth floors and a hole in the roof to let out the smoke. They rarely had windows, and never glass. Such furniture as there was, consisted of a rough table and stools, and a few earthenware bowls or jugs served for all purposes. Each man or woman carried a knife which, assisted by the fingers, took the place of our knives, forks and spoons.

The nobles, though they never starved, lived in conditions which we would consider unfit today. In a period when any man might attack his neighbour at any time, castles were built for defence, not comfort. No house or castle contained a bath and even in the King's palaces the floors were covered with rushes. When these were foul with dirt, clean rushes were strewn on top of them.

The whole country was bitterly discontented. Nobles and commoners alike rebelled against the harsh taxes imposed upon them by the King.

After having been on the throne for fifteen years, John found himself without a friend in the country. Hated alike by the clergy, the nobles and the common people, he now did a most foolish thing. Instead of trying to improve the living conditions of the people, he made them infinitely worse.

Hiring a number of soldiers from the continent, he marched north to revenge himself on the northern nobles who had refused to accompany him to France. The hired mercenaries cared nothing for England or the English people. Wherever they went they terrorised the countryside, burning and looting the farms and villages. In his insane rage John encouraged them to do their worst.

The brave Archbishop Langton followed the army to Northampton. There he boldly faced the King and accused him of violating the oath he had taken at his coronation, when he had solemnly sworn to protect the people of his realm.

"Mind your church," shouted John, "and leave me to govern the country!" The Archbishop was not to be so easily put off. A second time, at Nottingham, he stood before the King, warning him that he would again be excommunicated if he continued in his evil ways.

John was frightened. He remembered what had happened before, and how he had had to humble himself to the Papal Legate. He agreed to confer with the nobles in council.

Langton returned to London and met the nobles, who were already plotting against the King. He persuaded them that although they might win a civil war, the whole country would suffer. It would be much better to draw up a charter of liberties, force the King to sign it, and see to it that he kept his promise.

The nobles were doubtful. None of them trusted King John. It was only when Archbishop Langton produced a forgotten document, a Charter of Liberties granted by Henry I, that they agreed.

It was determined that a new Charter should be drawn up, based on the one which the Archbishop had read to them. In November, 1214, all the nobles and barons met at Bury St. Edmunds. One by one they knelt at the altar in the great church and vowed to take arms against the King if he refused to grant the new Charter. Archbishop Langton watched them with grim satisfaction. At last, he thought, the country would have good government.

At Christmas, John attended a gathering of the Great Council at Worcester. It is interesting for those who live in Worcester today to try to imagine what such a gathering must have looked like, there and in a score of towns up and down the country.

Today our towns are filled with noisy traffic and people in drab-coloured clothes. The nobles of the thirteenth century would have made a colourful picture as they thronged the narrow streets with their retainers and servants.

Some of them, nervous of what might be the outcome, would be in armour, with gay coloured surcoats. Others would be wearing long gowns, called cottes, reaching to their ankles. Over them they wore surcoats with long loose sleeves, lined and decorated with fur. All would be in gay colours and rich materials.

It is very certain that John did not greet them pleasantly. As he sat scowling on his throne, he tried to gain time. Treacherous as ever, he promised to meet them at Easter, at the same time sending a secret message to the Pope, pleading for his help. However, there was nothing that the Pope could do: when John offered to submit the dispute to Rome, the nobles refused.

Advised by the wise Archbishop, the nobles had realised that the quarrel with the King was a matter which concerned everybody. They made sure of the support of the Lord Mayor and the citizens of London, as well as the burghers of towns and cities all over the country.

From the shires yeomen and freemen, equally opposed to the King, gathered at Stamford at Easter. They found the nobles waiting with 2,000 armed knights. John was at Oxford with his foreign mercenaries.

The nobles submitted their claims to the King, and we are told that his fury was terrible to see. "You wish to take away my crown and make a slave of me!" he shouted. The nobles looked on unmoved. With 2,000 knights at their command, they had nothing but scorn for the King's rage.

Bidding him think it over, they marched to London. Everywhere they were received as saviours of the country. John retired to Odiham, and in a further attempt to gain time, he sent the Earl of Pembroke to try to spread disaffection amongst them. They replied that they would meet the King at Runnymede, a meadow by the River Thames, on June 15th, 1215.

It is more than probable that John did not mean to keep his promise to meet the nobles. He looked round vainly for help, but found none. Even the few remaining followers began to leave him. Soon only seven knights remained faithful to him.

During the weeks between Easter and the date in June, the King sat day after day biting his nails in silent fury. We are told that this was a bad habit which he had acquired as a boy and had never lost. If it had been his only bad habit, he would not have been in the situation in which he now found himself.

Meanwhile the Great Charter, known always by its Latin name as Magna Carta, was being drawn up by what we would today call a committee of nobles, churchmen and leading citizens.

With the exception of the monks, very few people in the country could read in 1215. Certainly none of the barons would have been able to read the terms of the charter which they were to present to the King. Nor could he. It is doubtful whether any English king, except Alfred the Great, could read until about the time of Richard II.

Runnymede is a name which means a great deal to every citizen not only in Great Britain, but also in the United States of America.

It is in fact a marshy piece of land by the Thames, between Staines and Windsor. King John was on one bank, and the nobles, led by Archbishop Langton, were on the other. When the King was rowed across to a neutral island between the two, he found twenty-five armed men grimly waiting to receive him.

Magna Carta, the Great Charter of English liberties, was ready for the royal seal. When the Archbishop presented it to him, King John received it with a scowl. But one look at the armed men made him realise that for the moment he had no choice. He still hoped to gain time, and we are told that all day there were discussions and arguments. It was not until nightfall that John affixed his seal to the Charter.

When the King returned to his castle of Windsor, it is said that he was almost insane with rage. He insisted that he had only agreed under duress, a word which means something done unwillingly under the threat of violence. He shouted that the Charter was "mere foolishness" and he had no intention of keeping his promises.

There are four copies of Magna Carta in existence: in the British Museum, and in the cathedrals of Lincoln and Salisbury. They are amongst the most important documents in the history of our country.

Magna Carta consists of sixty-three different clauses. Most of them have very little to do with us today. They were inserted to protect the rights of the Church and the nobles against the King. There is, however, one clause which is the foundation of the liberty of every free citizen.

This is the section or, as it was called, the chapter, number 39. It states that "no freeman shall be taken or imprisoned except by the lawful judgment of his peers or by the law of the land." The illustration shows a typical trial taking place after Magna Carta.

We are so accustomed today to the honesty and fairness of British justice that it is difficult for us to realise what this meant in England seven hundred and fifty years ago. In those days no man's life or goods were safe. He could be taxed or imprisoned at the pleasure of the King, and there was nothing he could do about it. English kings since John's time have occasionally broken the terms of Magna Carta, but never recklessly.

The end of King John is soon told. When he had recovered from his rage he broke all the promises he had made at Runnymede.

Gathering an army of foreign mercenaries, he determined to take a final vengeance on the nobles who had forced him to consent to the terms of the Charter. He appealed to the Pope to release him from his oath and, marching north, he laid waste the country. Thousands of innocent people who had nothing to do with the Magna Carta, suffered from his fury. It is said that every morning he himself set fire to the house in which he had slept the night before.

The country was fast becoming a wilderness. The nobles even went to the length of inviting the son of the French King to cross the Channel and accept the English crown. He actually landed with a French army and entered London in triumph.

John retreated northwards. As he crossed what is now called the Wash, the rising tide destroyed all his baggage waggons together with the Crown Jewels and the money with which to pay his soldiers. As these were mercenaries, they saw no reason why they should remain in the service of a king who was no longer able to pay them. Without their help, John was powerless.

King John rode on, via Sleaford to Newark, hated, despised and, what hurt him most, utterly penniless. He knew that his end was near. On a miserable day in October, wet through and along roads deep in mud, this worst of English kings looked his last on the country which he had consistently betrayed. At Newark he died, possibly by poison. England was well rid of him.

The freedoms enjoyed by the inhabitants both of Great Britain and of the great English-speaking United States of America, owe a common debt of gratitude to what happened at Runnymede on that day in June, so long ago.

Those who in the seventeenth century sailed in the "Mayflower," although they had religious reasons for leaving England, had all grown up in a country where as citizens they were protected under Magna Carta. The rights and freedoms which their ancestors had won from King John they took with them to the New World: on them they based the laws under which their descendants live today.

Many millions of the citizens of the United States have probably never heard of Magna Carta. But if they were to go to Runnymede in England, they would find an acre of land which is American soil for ever, dedicated by Queen Elizabeth II on May 14th, 1965, as a token of our common heritage.

Serving woman

Lace-up Boot

Gentleman with Hawk

Gentleman's Shoe

Young girl

Singer

Troubadour

Sword and scabbard